EASY GUITAR
WITH NOTES & TAB

Disney

ENCANTO

Music from the Motion Picture Soundtrack
Original Songs by Lin-Manuel Miranda

ISBN 978-1-70516-366-5

Hal•Leonard®

Contact us:
Hal Leonard
7777 West Bluemound Road
Milwaukee, WI 53213
Email: info@halleonard.com

In Europe, contact:
Hal Leonard Europe Limited
42 Wigmore Street
Marylebone, London, W1U 2RY
Email: info@halleonardeurope.com

In Australia, contact:
Hal Leonard Australia Pty. Ltd.
4 Lentara Court
Cheltenham, Victoria, 3192 Australia
Email: info@halleonard.com.au

STRUM AND PICK PATTERNS

This chart contains the suggested strum and pick patterns that are referred to by number at the beginning of each song in this book. The symbols ⊓ and ∨ in the strum patterns refer to down and up strokes, respectively. The letters in the pick patterns indicate which right-hand fingers play which strings.

p = thumb
i = index finger
m = middle finger
a = ring finger

For example; Pick Pattern 2
is played: thumb - index - middle - ring

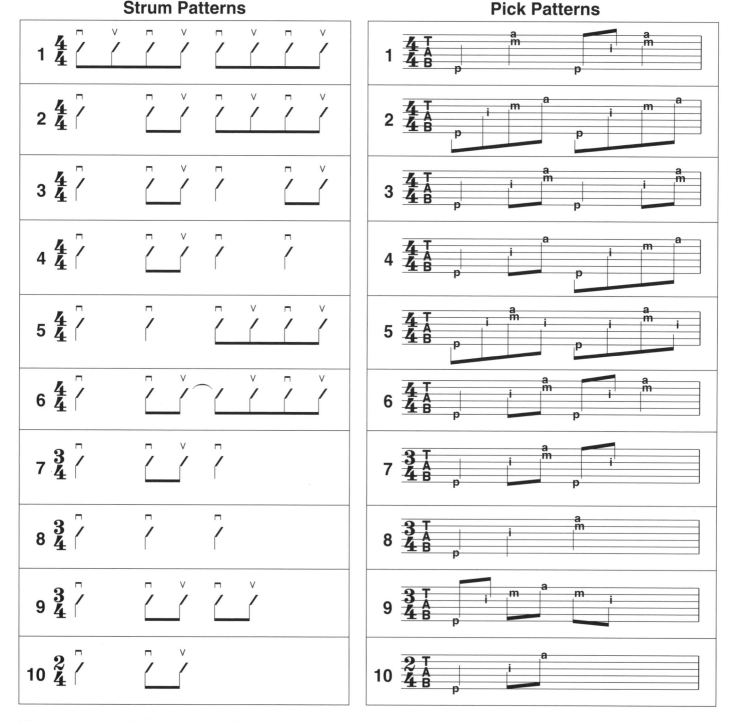

Strum Patterns   **Pick Patterns**

You can use the 3/4 Strum and Pick Patterns in songs written in compound meter (6/8, 9/8, 12/8, etc.). For example, you can accompany a song in 6/8 by playing the 3/4 pattern twice in each measure. The 4/4 Strum and Pick Patterns can be used for songs written in cut time (₵) by doubling the note time values in the patterns. Each pattern would therefore last two measures in cut time.

The Family Madrigal

Music and Lyrics by Lin-Manuel Miranda

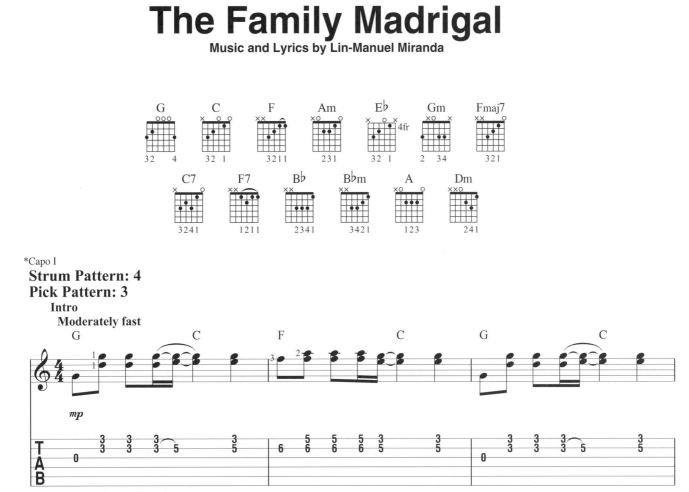

*Capo I

Strum Pattern: 4
Pick Pattern: 3

Intro
Moderately fast

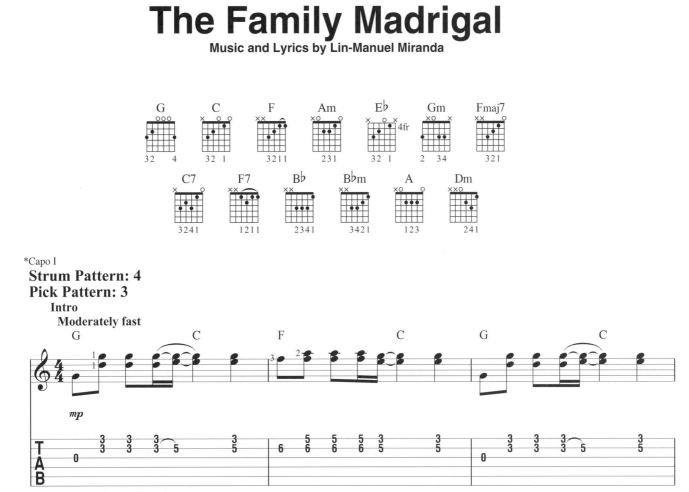

*Optional: To match recording, place capo at 1st fret.

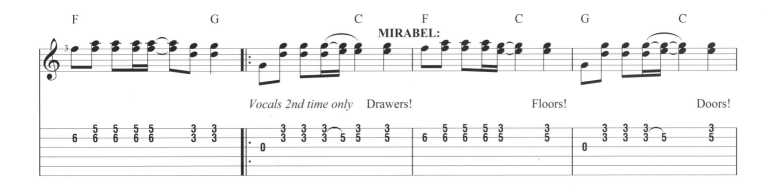

MIRABEL:

Vocals 2nd time only   Drawers!   Floors!   Doors!

Verse

Let's goooo!

1. This is our home, We've got ev-'ry gen-er-a-tion.
2. My *tí - a* Pe - pa—Her mood af - fects the weath - er.

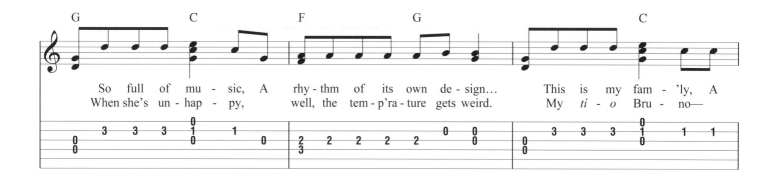

So full of mu - sic, A rhy - thm of its own de - sign... This is my fam - 'ly, A
When she's un - hap - py, well, the tem - p'ra - ture gets weird. My *tí - o* Bru - no—

per - fect con - stel - la - tion. So man - y stars, and __ ev - 'ry - bod - y gets to shine.
We don't talk a - bout Bru - no! They say he saw the fu - ture, __ One day he dis - ap - peared.

Pre-Chorus

MIRABEL (TOWNSPEOPLE):

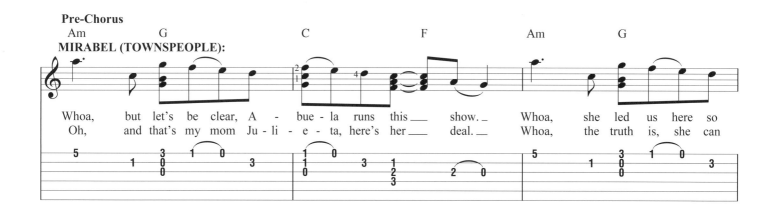

Whoa, but let's be clear, A - bue - la runs this __ show. _ Whoa, she led us here so
Oh, and that's my mom Ju - li - e - ta, here's her __ deal. _ Whoa, the truth is, she can

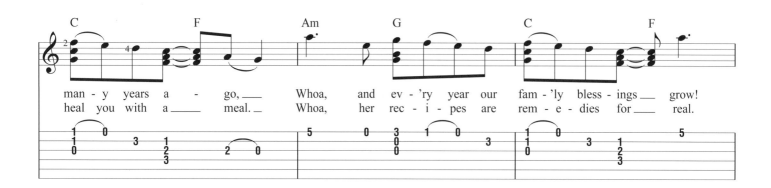

man - y years a - go, __ Whoa, and ev - 'ry year our fam - 'ly bless - ings __ grow!
heal you with a __ meal. _ Whoa, her rec - i - pes are rem - e - dies for __ real.

There's just a lot ___ you've sim-ply got to know, so... Wel-come _ to the Fam - 'ly Mad-ri - gal.
If you're im - pressed, _ i - ma-gine how I feel—Mom?! Wel-come _ to the Fam - 'ly Mad-ri - gal.

The home _ of the Fam - 'ly Mad - ri - gal. We're on our way! Where all ___ the peo-ple are fan -
The home _ of the Fam - 'ly Mad - ri - gal. Hey, com - ing through! I know _ it sounds a bit fan -

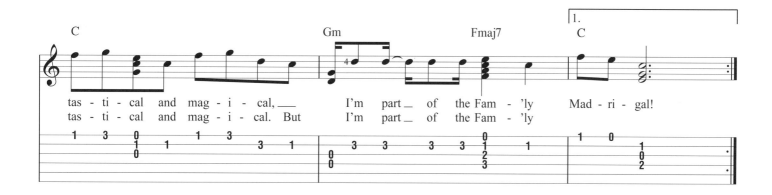

tas - ti - cal and mag - i - cal, ___ I'm part _ of the Fam - 'ly Mad - ri - gal!
tas - ti - cal and mag - i - cal. But I'm part _ of the Fam - 'ly

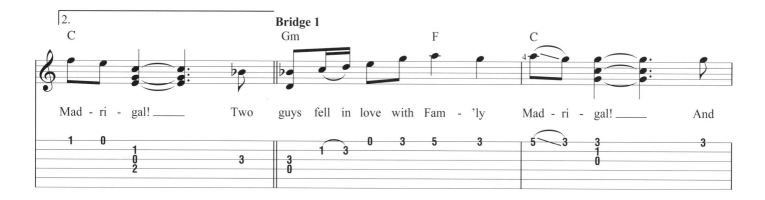

Mad - ri - gal! ___ Two guys fell in love with Fam - 'ly Mad - ri - gal! ___ And

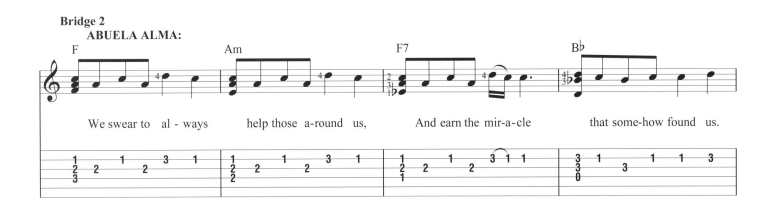

Bridge 2

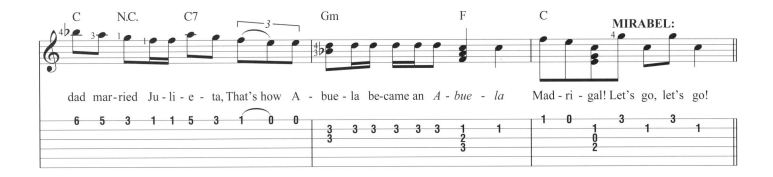

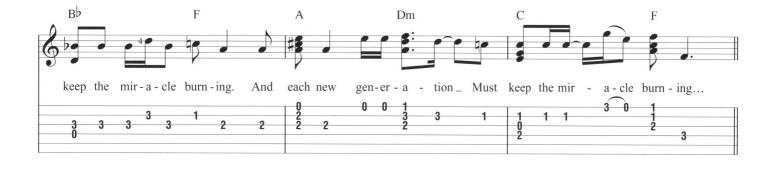

keep the mir - a - cle burn - ing. And each new gen - er - a - tion_ Must keep the mir - a - cle burn - ing...

Interlude

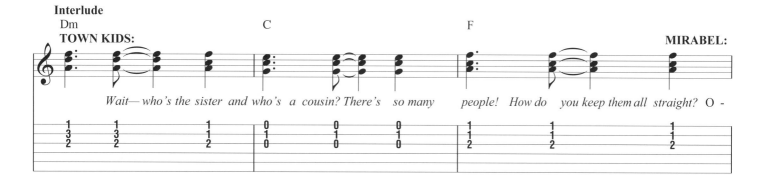

TOWN KIDS:

MIRABEL:

Wait— who's the sister and who's a cousin? There's so many people! How do you keep them all straight? O -

kay, o-kay, o-kay, o - kay... So man-y kids in our house, so let's turn the sound up! You know why? I think it's time for a

Verse

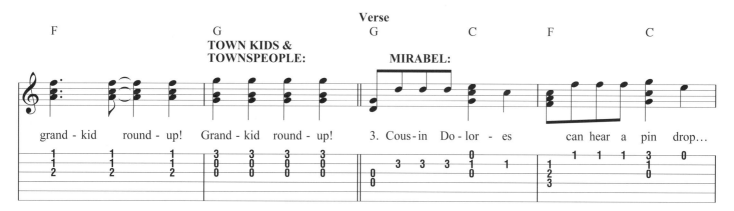

TOWN KIDS & TOWNSPEOPLE:

MIRABEL:

grand - kid round - up! Grand - kid round up! 3. Cous-in Do - lor - es can hear a pin drop...

Ca - mi - lo shape shifts, An - ton - i - o gets_ his gift to - day! My old - er sis - ers,

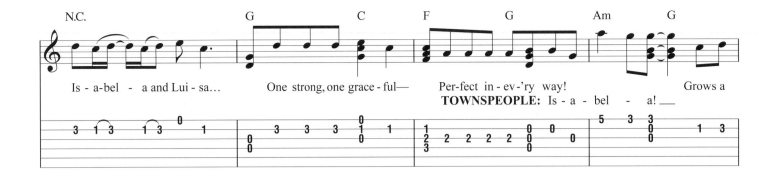

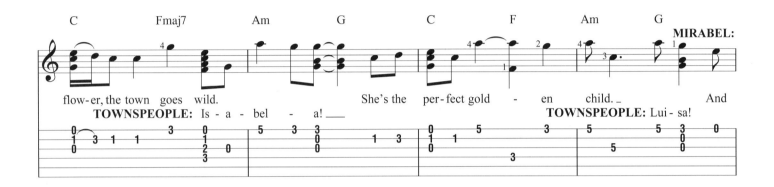

Chorus

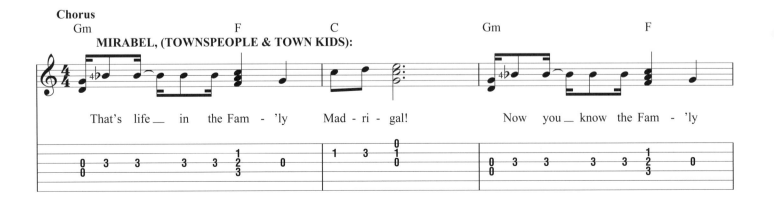

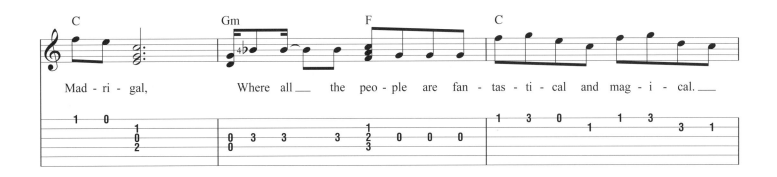

Mad - ri - gal, Where all __ the peo - ple are fan - tas - ti - cal and mag - i - cal. __

That's who we are in the Fam - 'ly... Mad - ri - gal! ¡Adios! Ooo! Ha!

TOWN KID: *But what's your gift?*

**MIRABEL,
(TOWNSPEOPLE
& TOWN KIDS):**

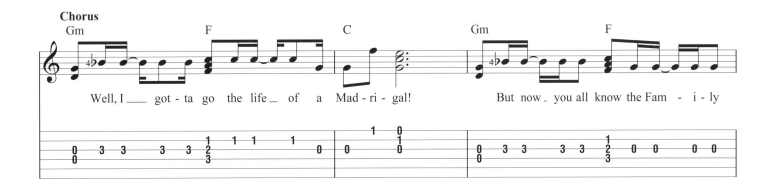

Chorus

Well, I __ got - ta go the life __ of a Mad - ri - gal! But now __ you all know the Fam - i - ly

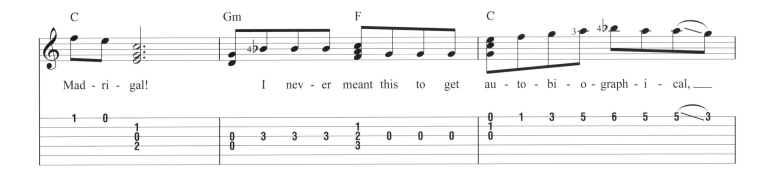

Mad - ri - gal! I nev - er meant this to get au - to - bi - o - graph - i - cal, __

So just _ to re-view, the Fam - i - ly Mad - ri - gal, let's go...

It starts with A - bue - la, and
My mom Ju - li - e - ta, can

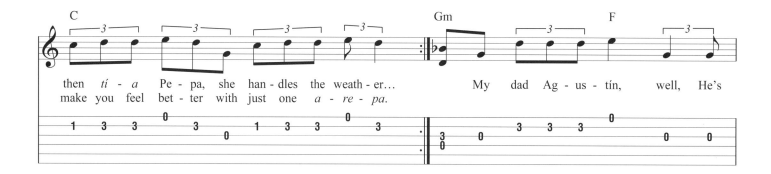

then *tí - a* Pe - pa, she han - dles the weath - er...
make you feel bet - ter with just one *a - re - pa.*

My dad Ag - us - tín, well, He's

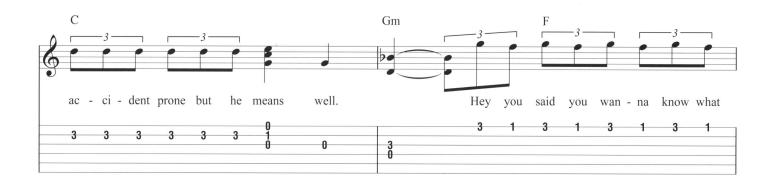

ac - ci - dent prone but he means well.

Hey you said you wan - na know what

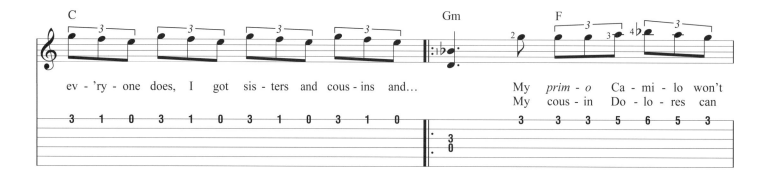

ev - 'ry - one does, I got sis - ters and cous - ins and...

My *prim - o* Ca - mi - lo won't
My cous - in Do - lo - res can

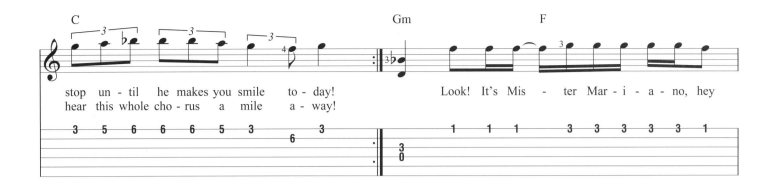

stop un - til he makes you smile to - day!
hear this whole cho - rus a mile a - way!
Look! It's Mis - ter Mar - i - a - no, hey

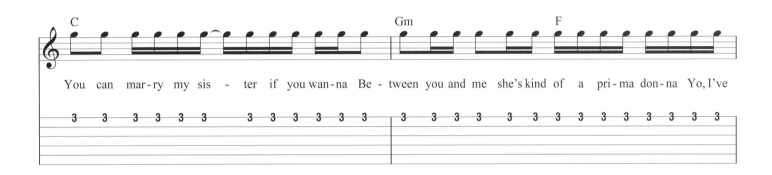

You can mar - ry my sis - ter if you wan - na Be - tween you and me she's kind of a pri - ma don - na Yo, I've

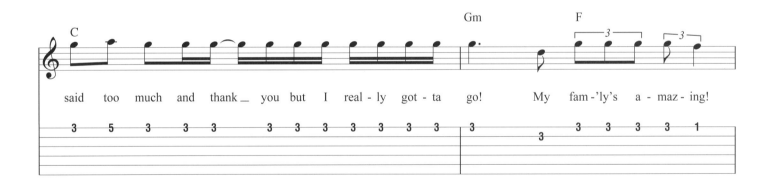

said too much and thank __ you but I real - ly got - ta go! My fam - 'ly's a - maz - ing!

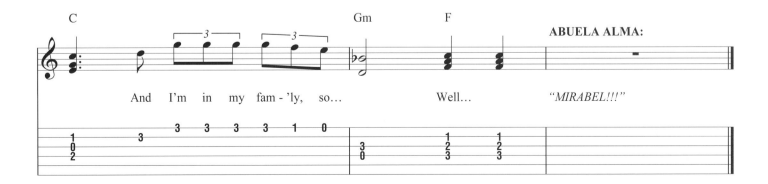

And I'm in my fam - 'ly, so... Well... **ABUELA ALMA:** *"MIRABEL!!!"*

Waiting On A Miracle

Music and Lyrics by Lin-Manuel Miranda

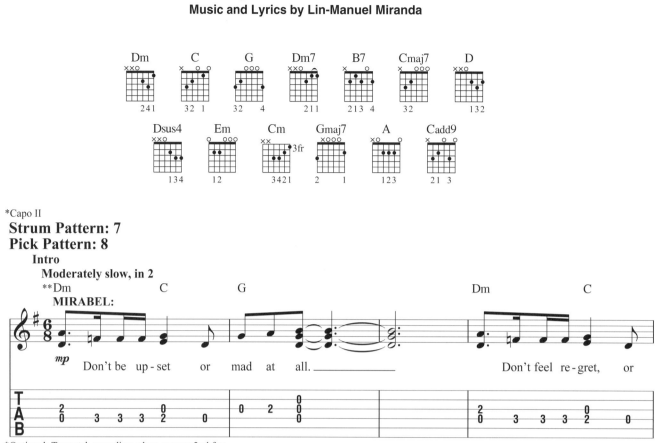

*Capo II

Strum Pattern: 7

Pick Pattern: 8

Intro

Moderately slow, in 2

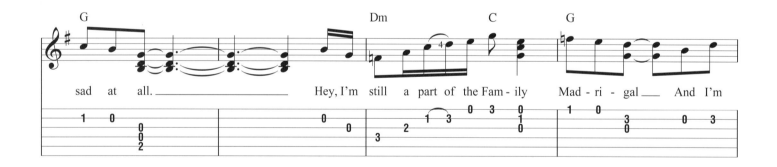

*Optional: To match recording, place capo at 2nd fret.

**Let chords ring throughout Intro.

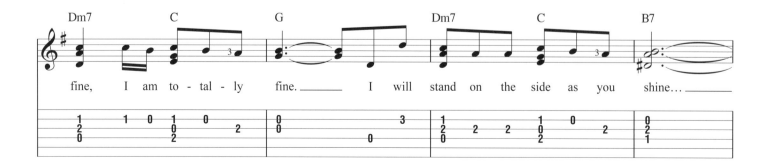

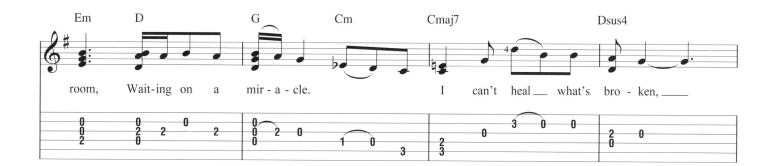

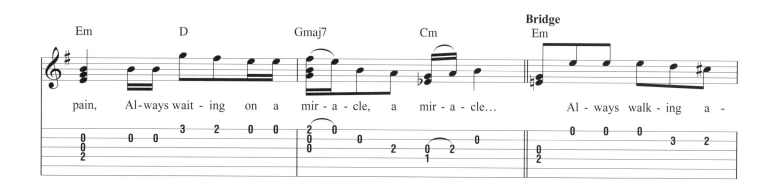

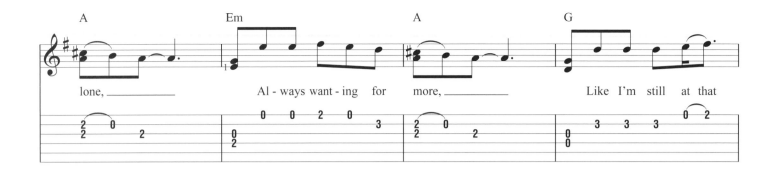

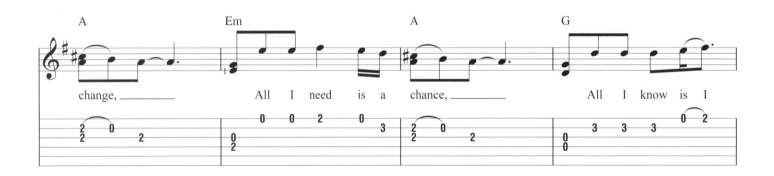

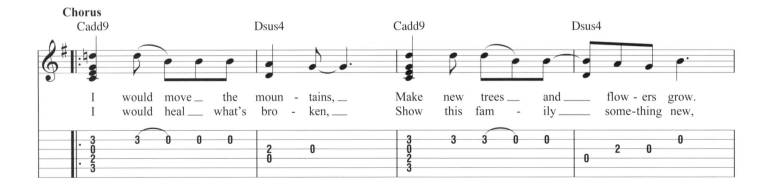

Some-one please_ just let me know Where do I go, I am wait-ing on a mir-a-cle, A mir-a-cle.
Who I am__ in - side._ So what can I

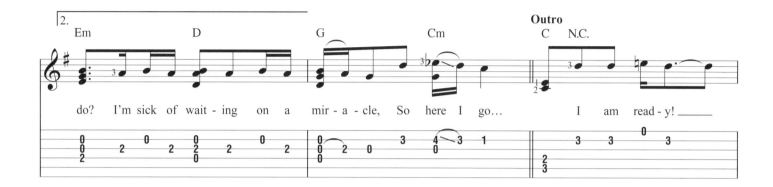

do? I'm sick of wait - ing on a mir - a-cle, So here I go... I am read - y!_____

C - 'mon, I'm read - y!_____ I've been pa - tient and stead - fast and stead - y!_____

Bless me now_ as you blessed us all those years a - go, When you gave us a

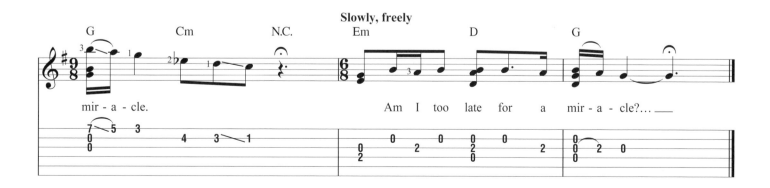

mir - a - cle. Am I too late for a mir - a - cle?... __

Surface Pressure

Music and Lyrics by Lin-Manuel Miranda

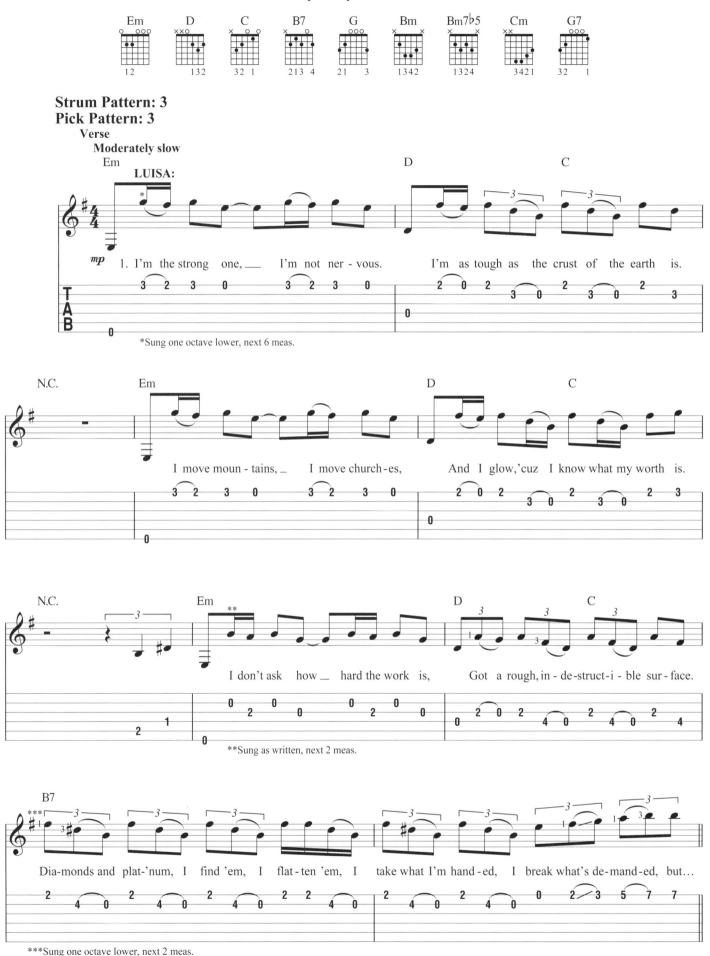

Strum Pattern: 3
Pick Pattern: 3

*Sung one octave lower, next 6 meas.

**Sung as written, next 2 meas.

***Sung one octave lower, next 2 meas.

Verse

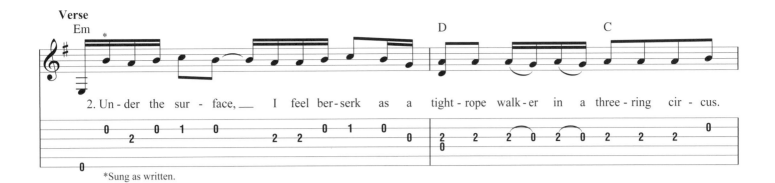

2. Un - der the sur - face, __ I feel ber - serk as a tight - rope walk - er in a three - ring cir - cus.

*Sung as written.

Un - der the sur - face, __ was Her - cu - les ev - er like "Yo, I don't wan - na fight Cerb - erus?"

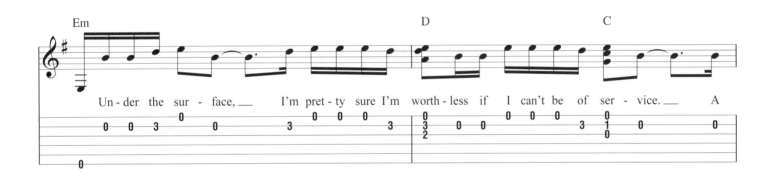

Un - der the sur - face, __ I'm pret - ty sure I'm worth - less if I can't be of ser - vice. __ A

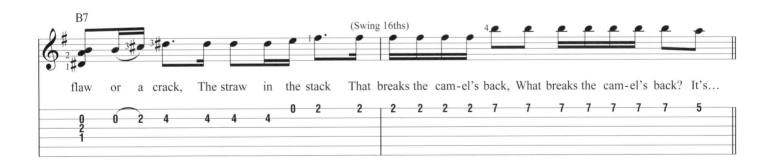

(Swing 16ths)

flaw or a crack, The straw in the stack That breaks the cam - el's back, What breaks the cam - el's back? It's…

𝄋 Chorus

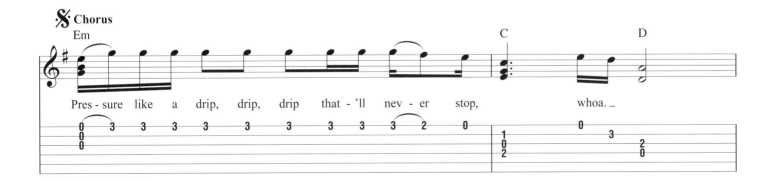

Pres - sure like a drip, drip, drip that - 'll nev - er stop, whoa. __

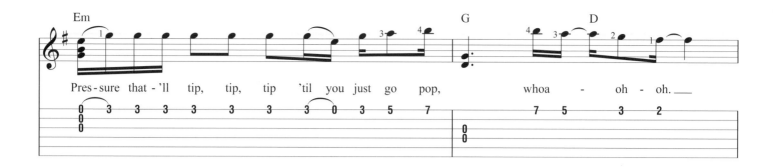

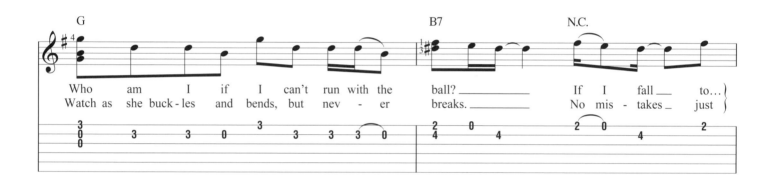

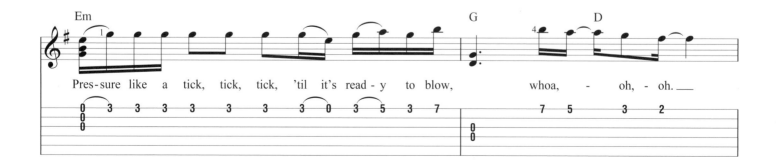

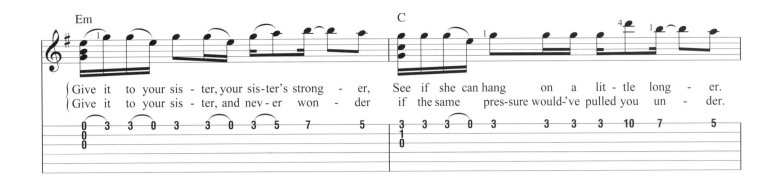

Give it to your sis - ter, your sis - ter's strong - er, See if she can hang on a lit - tle long - er.
Give it to your sis - ter, and nev - er won - der if the same pres-sure would-'ve pulled you un - der.

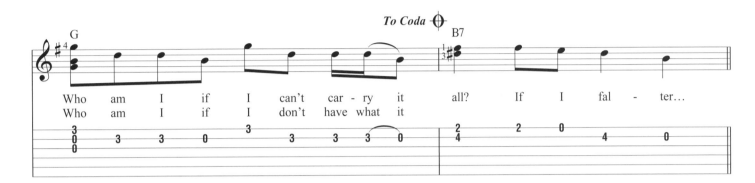

To Coda ⊕

Who am I if I can't car - ry it all? If I fal - ter...
Who am I if I don't have what it

Verse
(Straight 16ths)

3. Un - der the sur - face, ___ I hide my nerves, and it wor - sens, I wor - ry some-thing is gon - na hurt us.

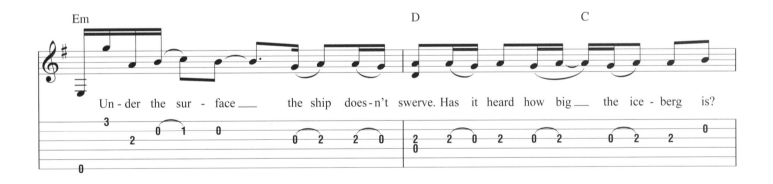

Un - der the sur - face ___ the ship does-n't swerve. Has it heard how big ___ the ice - berg is?

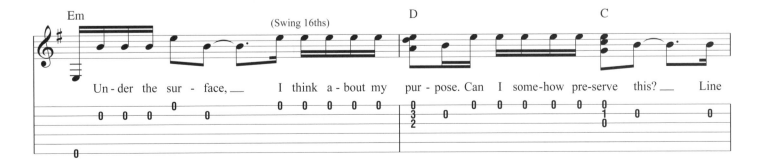

(Swing 16ths)

Un - der the sur - face, ___ I think a - bout my pur - pose. Can I some-how pre - serve this? ___ Line

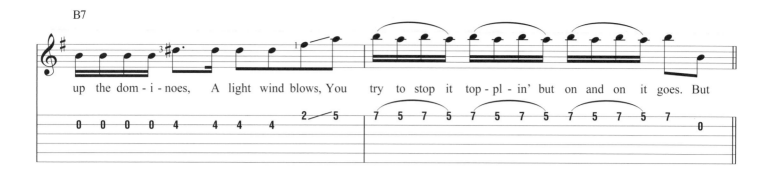

up the dom-i-noes, A light wind blows, You try to stop it top-pl-in' but on and on it goes. But

Bridge
(Straight 16ths)

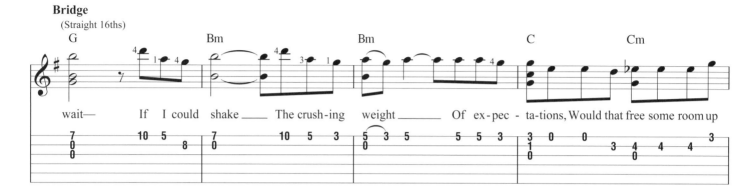

wait— If I could shake The crush-ing weight Of ex-pec-ta-tions, Would that free some room up

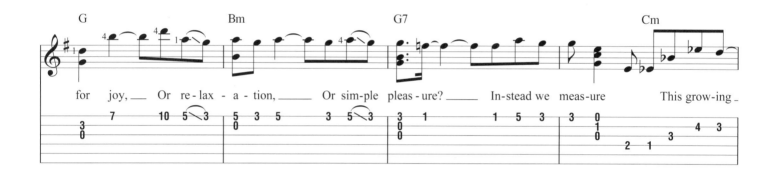

for joy, Or re-lax-a-tion, Or sim-ple pleas-ure? In-stead we meas-ure This grow-ing

D.S. al Coda
(Back to Swing 16ths)

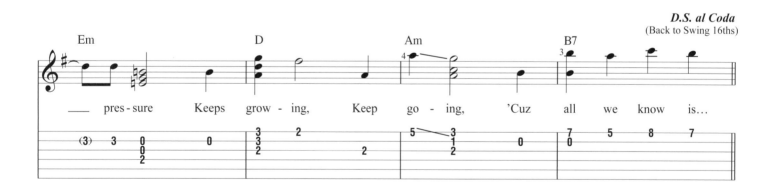

pres-sure Keeps grow-ing, Keep go-ing, 'Cuz all we know is...

Coda

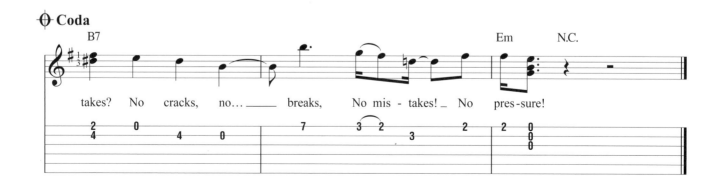

takes? No cracks, no... breaks, No mis-takes! No pres-sure!

Colombia, Mi Encanto

Music and Lyrics by Lin-Manuel Miranda

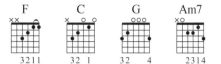

Strum Pattern: 4
Pick Pattern: 6

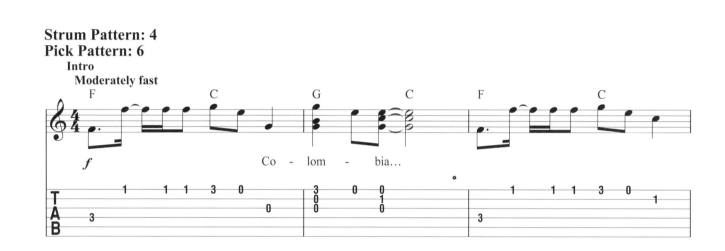

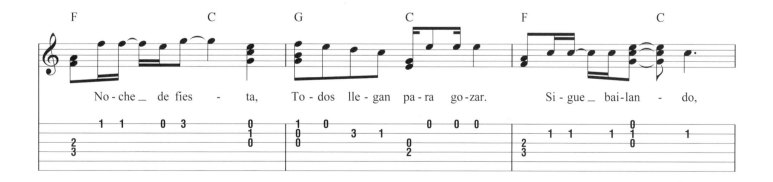

Con-ten - to en mi pa - ra - í - so,   Y re - ve-lan - do   Mi - la - gros en - ca - da pi - so.

(A -

*Sung together

Interlude

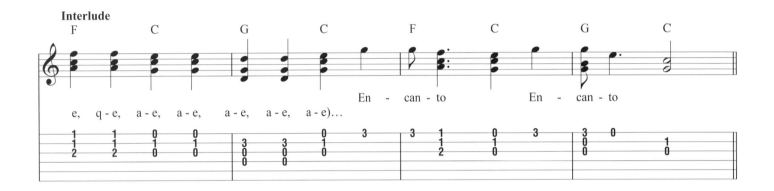

e,   q-e,   a-e,   a-e,   a-e,   a-e,   a-e)...   En - can - to   En - can - to

𝄋 Chorus

Co -lom - bia, te qui - e - ro   tan - to ___   Que siem - pre me en-a - mo - ra tu en -

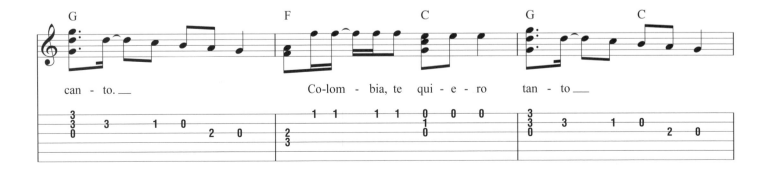

can - to. ___   Co-lom - bia, te qui-e - ro   tan - to ___

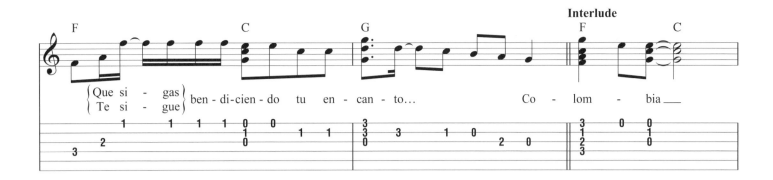

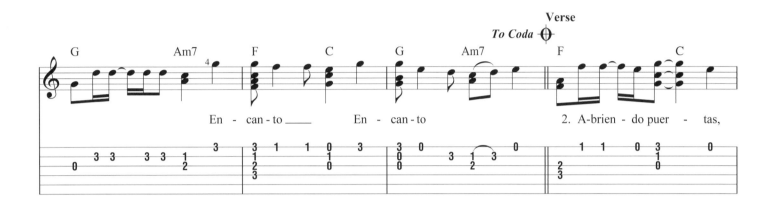

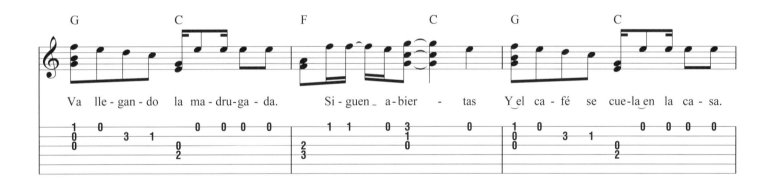

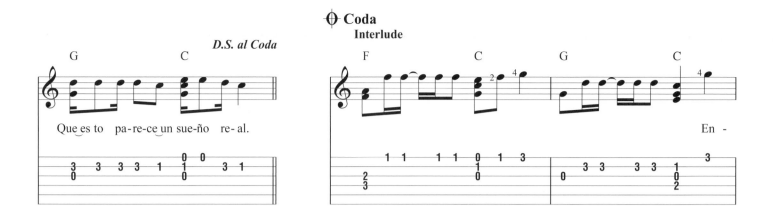

D.S. al Coda

G   **C**

Que es to pa-re-ce un sue-ño re-al.

Interlude

F   **C**   **G**   **C**

En -

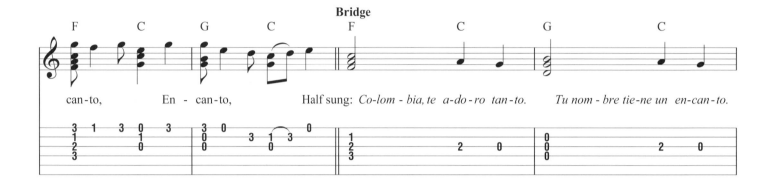

F   **C**   **G**   **C**   **Bridge** **F**   **C**   **G**   **C**

can-to,   En - can-to,   Half sung: *Co-lom - bia, te a-do-ro tan-to.*   *Tu nom - bre tie-ne un en-can-to.*

F   **C**   **G**   **C**   **F**   **C**

De Bo - go tá has-ta Pa-len-que   *Me fui con to-da la gen-te.*   Co-lom - bia, tie-rra tan be-lla,

G   **C**   **F**   **C**   **G** **N.C.**

La ma - dre na-tu-ra-le-za   Te dio un - a for-ma de ser. *Co-lom-bi-a stays my fa-vor-ite place.*

Chorus

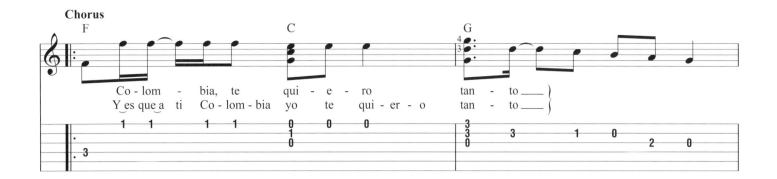

Co - lom - bia, te qui - e - ro tan - to ____

Y es que a ti Co - lom - bia yo te qui - er - o tan - to ____

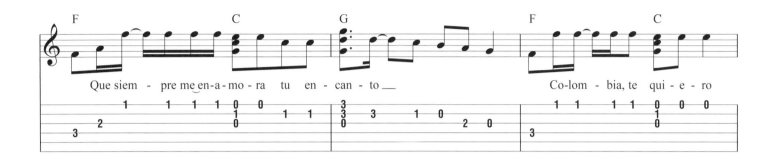

Que siem - pre me en-a - mo - ra tu en - can - to ___ Co-lom-bia, te qui-e-ro

tan - to ___ Te si - gue ben-di-cien - do tu en - can - to...

Outro

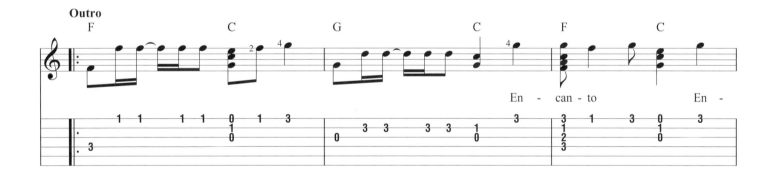

En - can - to En -

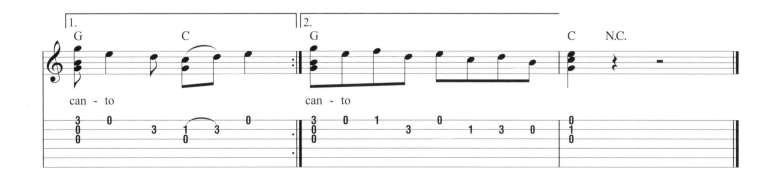

1. can - to

2. can - to

We Don't Talk About Bruno

Music and Lyrics by Lin-Manuel Miranda

*Capo III

Strum Pattern: 4

Pick Pattern: 4

Intro
Moderately

PEPA: We don't talk a-bout Bru - no, no, no, no! We don't talk a-bout Bru -

*Optional: To match recording, place capo at 3rd fret.

Verse

- no... 1. But, It was my wed-ding day, We were get-ting read-y, and there

FÉLIX: It was our wed-ding day...

PEPA:

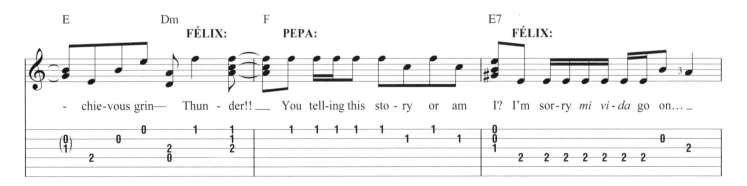

was-n't a cloud _ in the sky. No clouds al - lowed _ in the sky. Bru - no walks in ____ with a mis -

FÉLIX: PEPA:

- chie-vous grin— Thun - der!! ___ You tell-ing this sto - ry or am I? I'm sor - ry *mi vi-da* go on... _

FÉLIX:

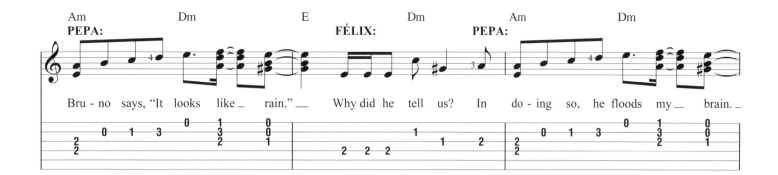

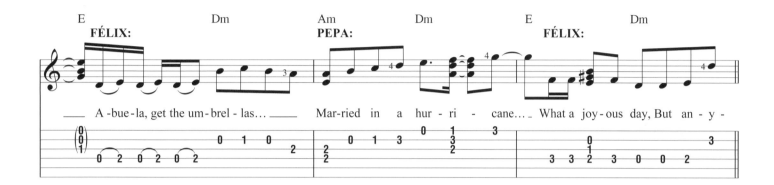

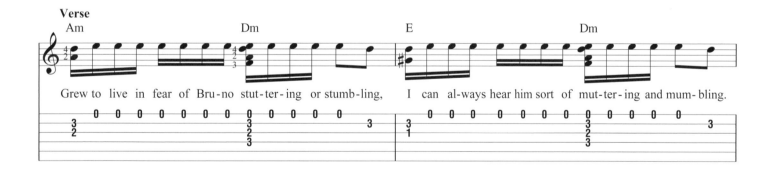

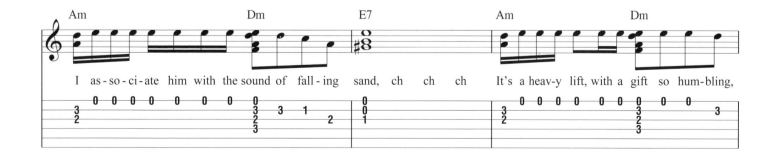

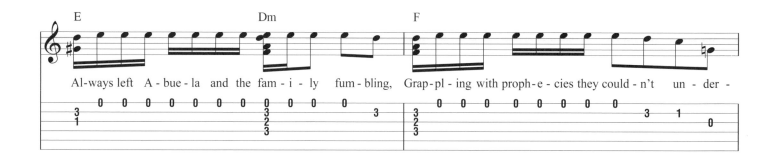

Al-ways left A - bue - la and the fam - i - ly fum - bling, Grap-pl - ing with proph - e - cies they could - n't un - der -

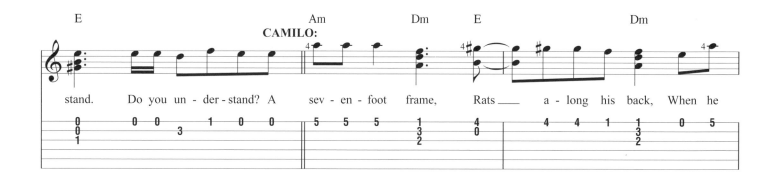

CAMILO:

stand. Do you un - der - stand? A sev - en - foot frame, Rats ___ a - long his back, When he

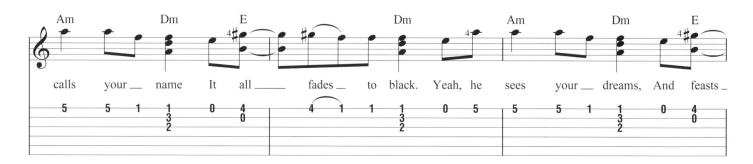

calls your ___ name It all ___ fades ___ to black. Yeah, he sees your ___ dreams, And feasts ___

Chorus

TOWNSPEOPLE **PEPA, FÉLIX,**
& TOWN KIDS: **CAMILO, DOLORES:**

___ on ___ your screams
Hey! We don't talk a - bout Bru - no, no, no, no! We don't talk a - bout Bru -

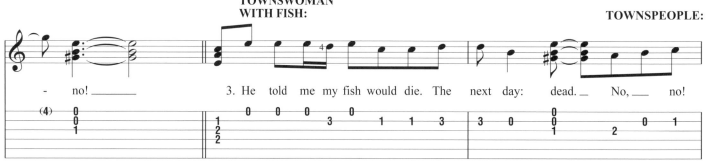

Verse

TOWNSWOMAN
WITH FISH:

TOWNSPEOPLE:

- no! ___ 3. He told me my fish would die. The next day: dead. ___ No, ___ no!

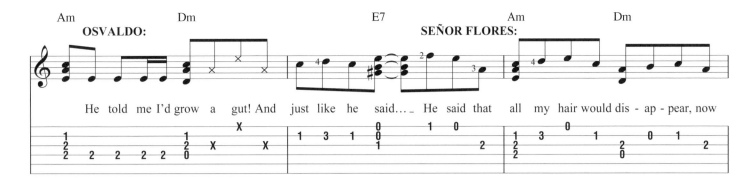

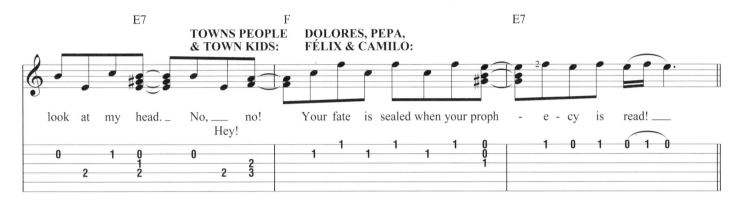

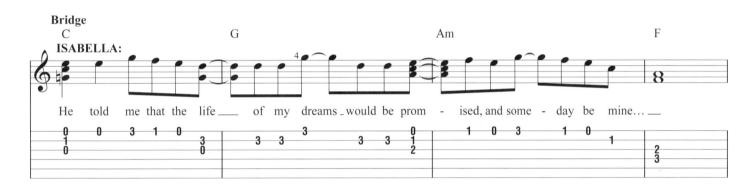

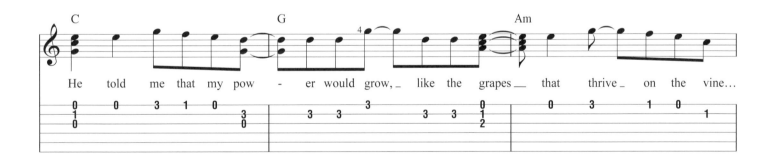

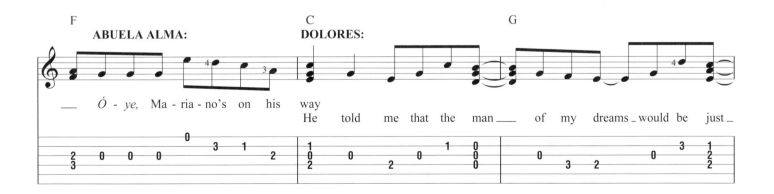

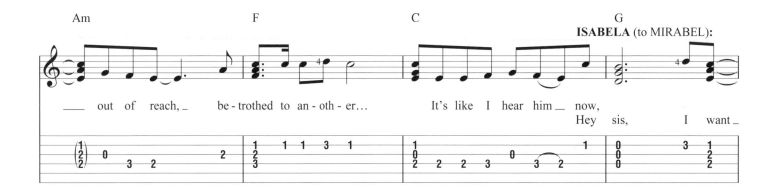

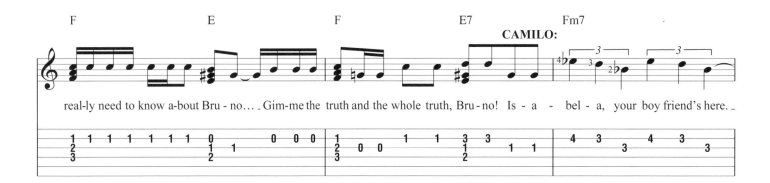

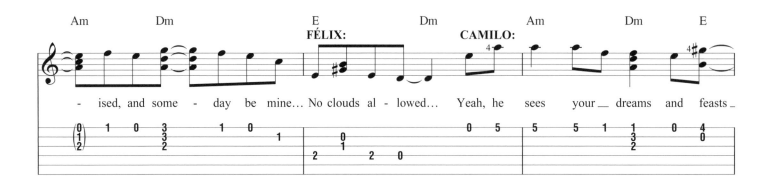

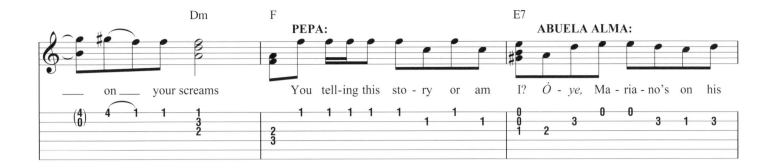

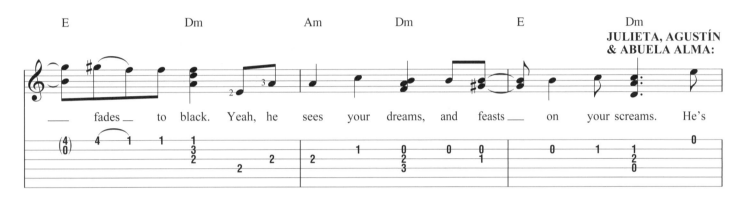

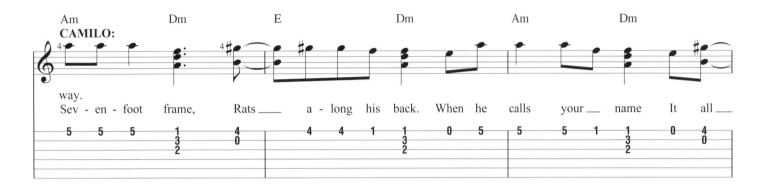

What Else Can I Do?

Music and Lyrics by Lin-Manuel Miranda

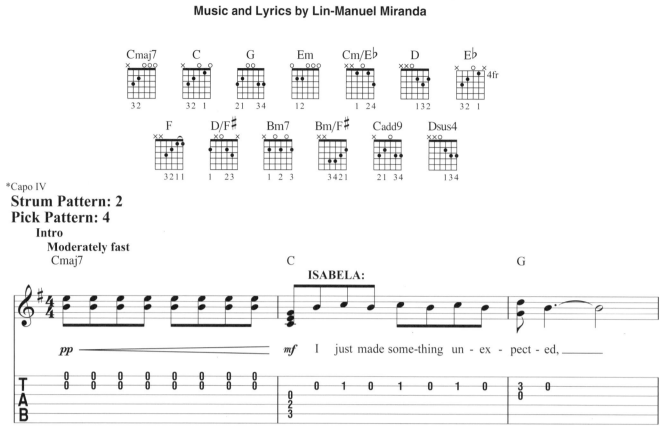

*Capo IV

Strum Pattern: 2
Pick Pattern: 4

Intro
Moderately fast

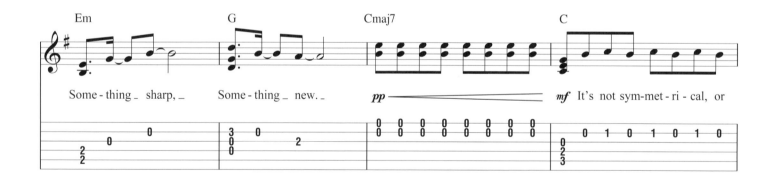

*Optional: To match recording, place capo at 4th fret.

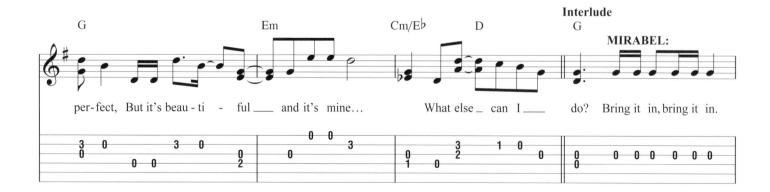

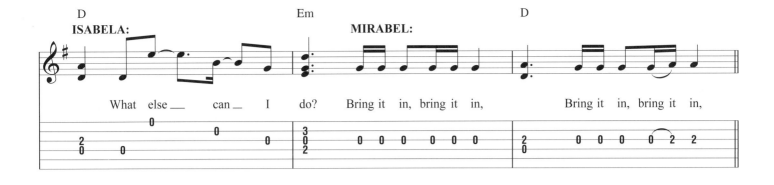

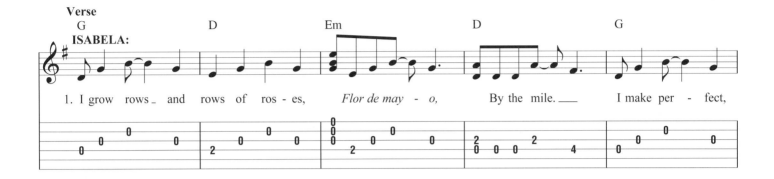

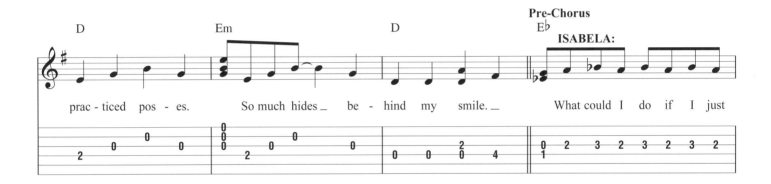

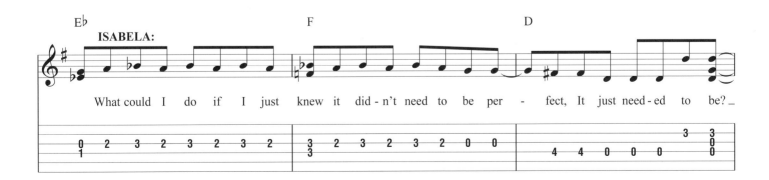

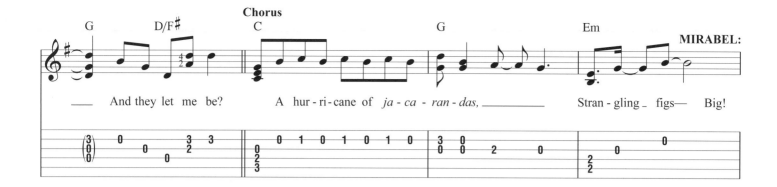

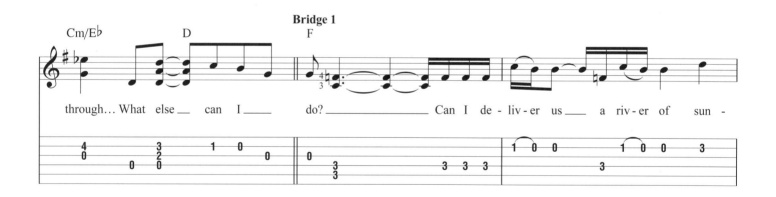

shiv-er of some - thing new. _____ I'm so sick of pret - ty, I want some-thing true, don't

Bridge 2

you?
You just seem Like your life's ___ been a dream, _ Since the mo - ment you o - pened your eyes.

How

far do these roots go down?
All I know Are the blos - soms you grow, _ but it's awe -

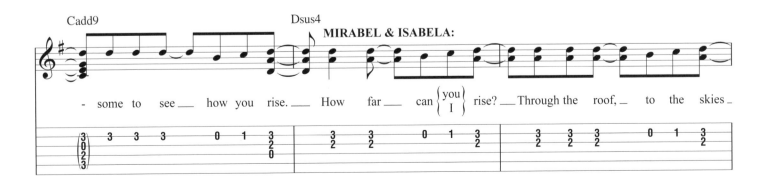

- some to see ___ how you rise. ___ How far ___ can {you / I} rise? ___ Through the roof, _ to the skies _

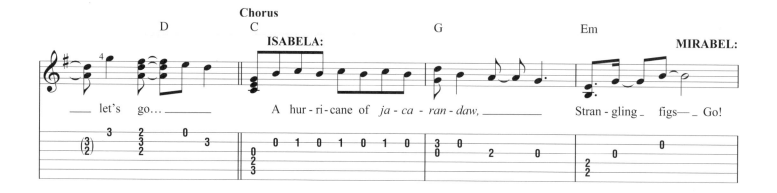

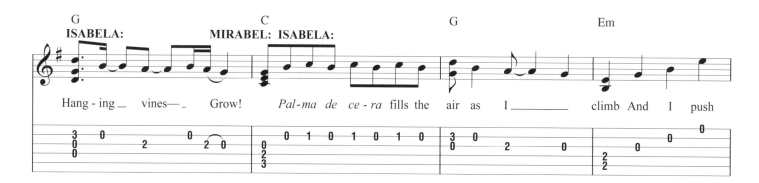

Chorus

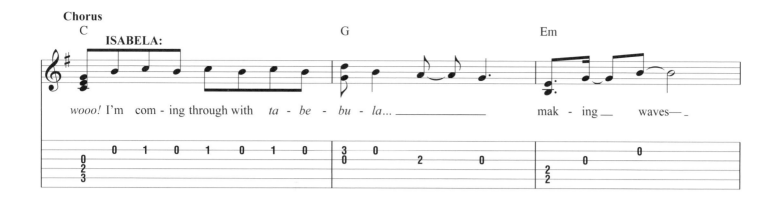

wooo! I'm com-ing through with *ta - be - bu - la...* _____ mak-ing __ waves__

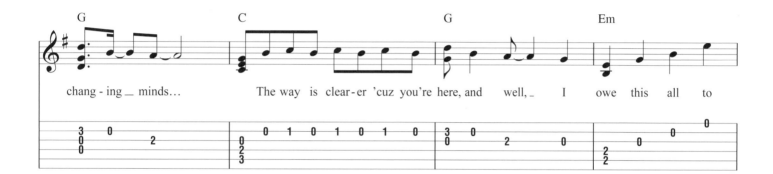

chang-ing __ minds... The way is clear-er 'cuz you're here, and well,_ I owe this all to

Outro

you. What else __ can I ____ do? ___ What else __ can I ____
Show 'em what you can do— __

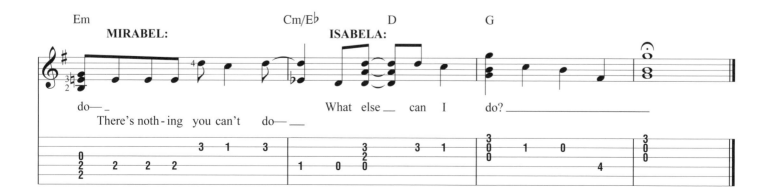

do— _ What else __ can I do? _____
There's noth-ing you can't do— __

Dos Oruguitas

Music and Lyrics by Lin-Manuel Miranda

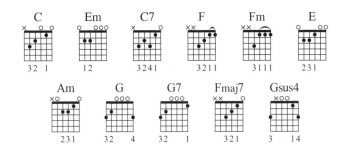

Strum Pattern: 4
Pick Pattern: 6

Intro
Moderately, in 2

Verse

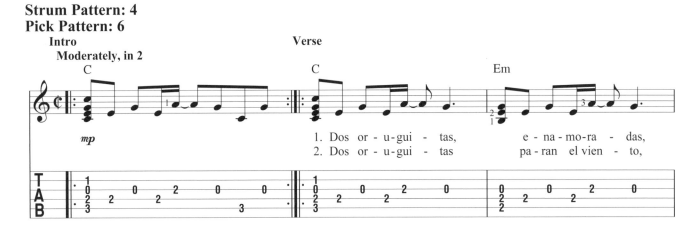

1. Dos or - u - gui - tas,   e - na - mo - ra - das,
2. Dos or - u - gui - tas   pa - ran el vien - to,

pa - san sus no - ches   y ma - dru - ga - das.   Lle - nas de ham - bre,
mien - tras se a - bra - zan   con sen - ti - mien - to.   Si - guen - cre - cien - do,

si - guen an - dan - do   y na - ve - gan - do un mun - do   que cam - bia, y si - gue cam - bian - do.
no sa - ben cuán - do   bu - scar al - gún__ rin - cón.   El tiem - po si - gue cam - bian - do.   In -

Na - ve - gan - do un mun - do que cam - bia, y si - gue cam - bian - do.
se - pa - ra - bles son, y el tiem - po si - gue cam - bian - do.

Chorus

Ay, __ or - u - gui - tas,

no __ se a - guan - ten más. Hay __ que cre - cer a - par - te y vol - ver, ha - cia a - de - lan - te se __ gui - rás.

Vie - nen mi - la - gros, vien - en cri - sá - li - das. Hay __ que par - tir y __ cons - tru -

Interlude

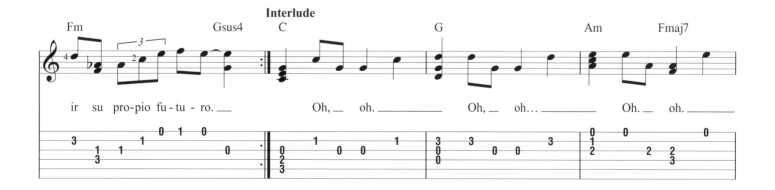

ir su pro - pio fu - tu - ro. __ Oh, __ oh. __ Oh, __ oh... __ Oh. __ oh. __

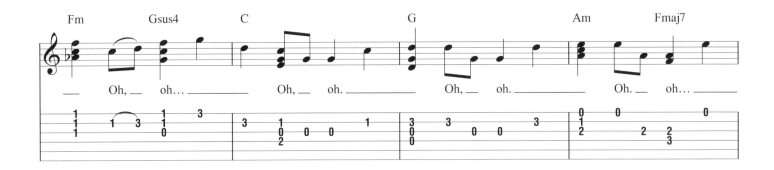

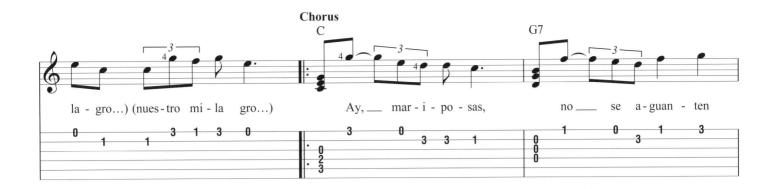

la - gro...) (nues - tro mi - la gro...)   Ay, ___ mar - i - po - sas,   no ___ se a - guan - ten

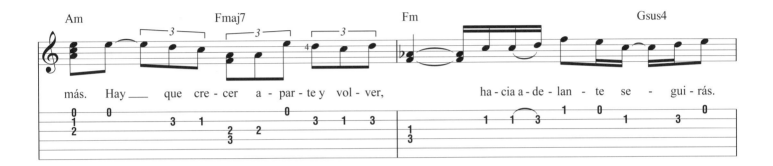

más. Hay ___ que cre - cer a - par - te y vol - ver,   ha - cia a - de - lan - te se - gui - rás.

Ya ___ son mi - la - gros   rom - pien - do cri - sá - li - das. Hay ___ que vo - lar, hay ___ que en - con-

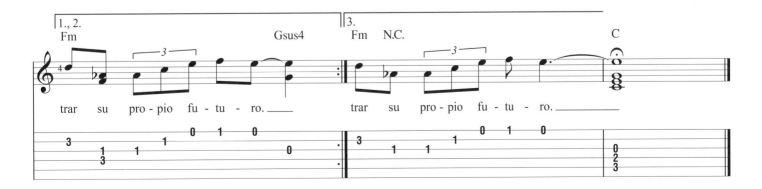

trar su pro - pio fu - tu - ro. ___   trar su pro - pio fu - tu - ro. ___

All Of You

Music and Lyrics by Lin-Manuel Miranda

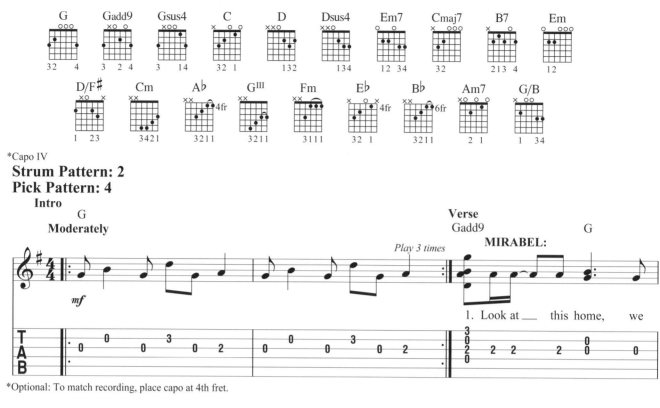

*Capo IV

Strum Pattern: 2
Pick Pattern: 4

*Optional: To match recording, place capo at 4th fret.

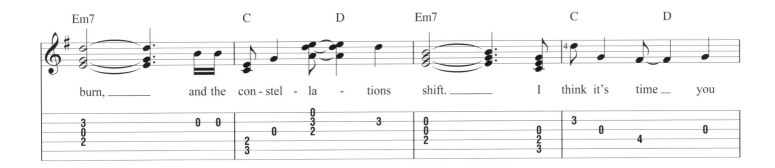

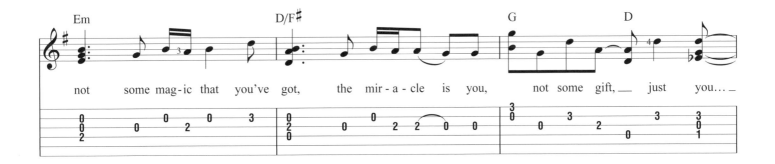

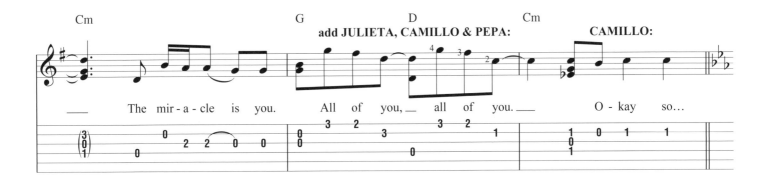

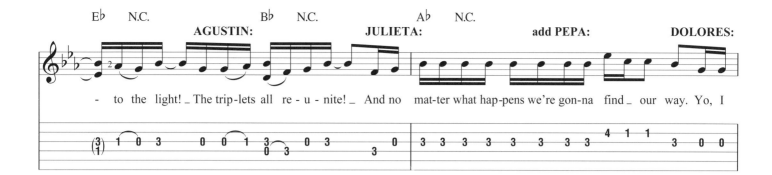

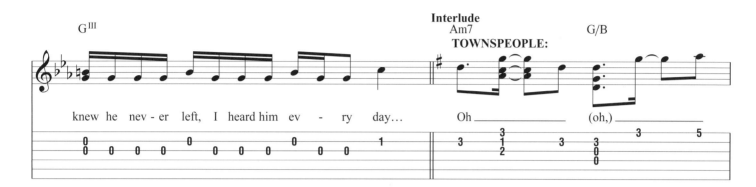

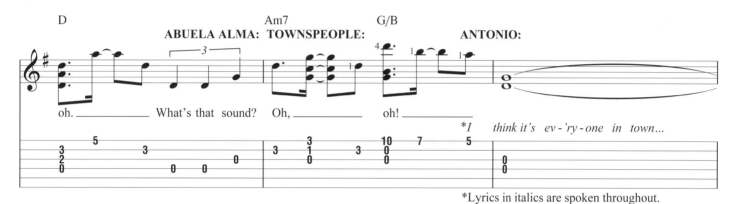

*Lyrics in italics are spoken throughout.

**Sung together

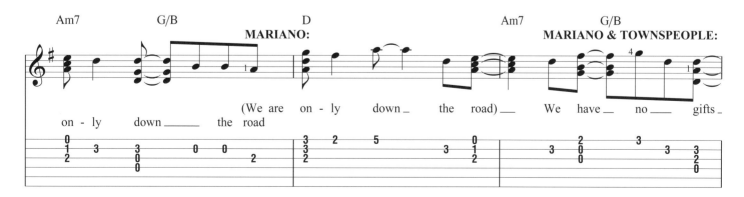

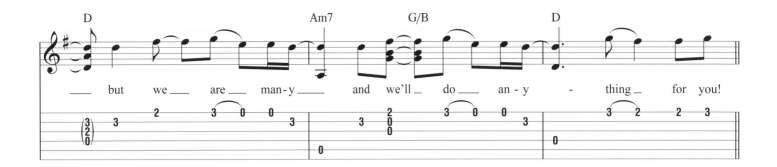

but we are man-y and we'll do an-y-thing for you!

Verse

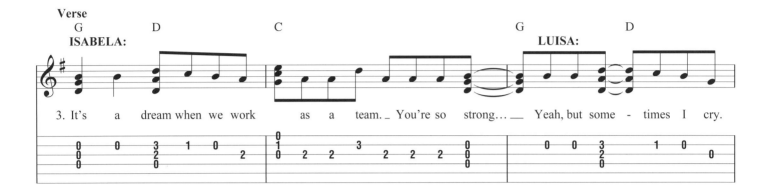

ISABELA:
3. It's a dream when we work as a team. You're so strong... Yeah, but some-times I cry.

MIRABEL & ISABELA: LUISA:
So do I! I may not be as strong, but I'm get-ting wis - er.

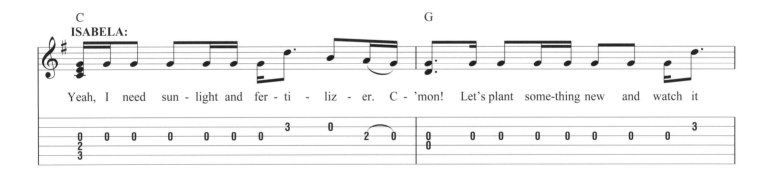

ISABELA:
Yeah, I need sun-light and fer-ti-liz-er. C-'mon! Let's plant some-thing new and watch it

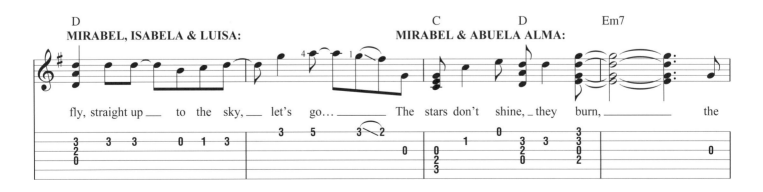

MIRABEL, ISABELA & LUISA: MIRABEL & ABUELA ALMA:
fly, straight up to the sky, let's go... The stars don't shine, they burn, the

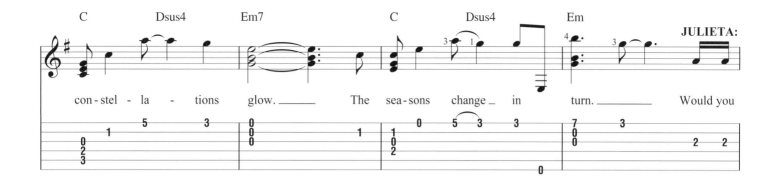

con-stel-la-tions glow._____ The sea-sons change_ in turn._____ Would you

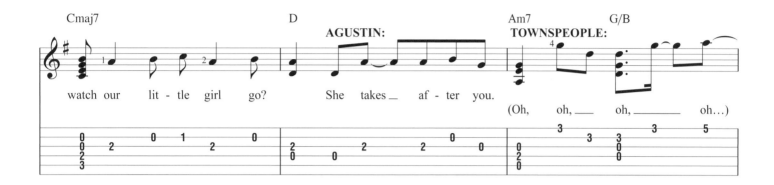

watch our lit-tle girl go? She takes_ af-ter you. (Oh, oh,__ oh,_____ oh...)

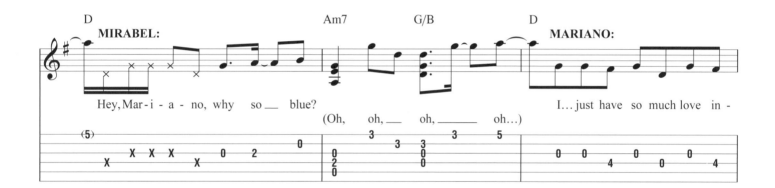

Hey, Mar-i-a-no, why so_ blue? (Oh, oh,__ oh,_____ oh...) I... just have so much love in-

side... (Oh,__ oh,_____ oh...) Y'know, I've got this cous-in too. Have you met Do-lor-es?

O-kay I'll take it from here, g'bye... You talk so loud, you

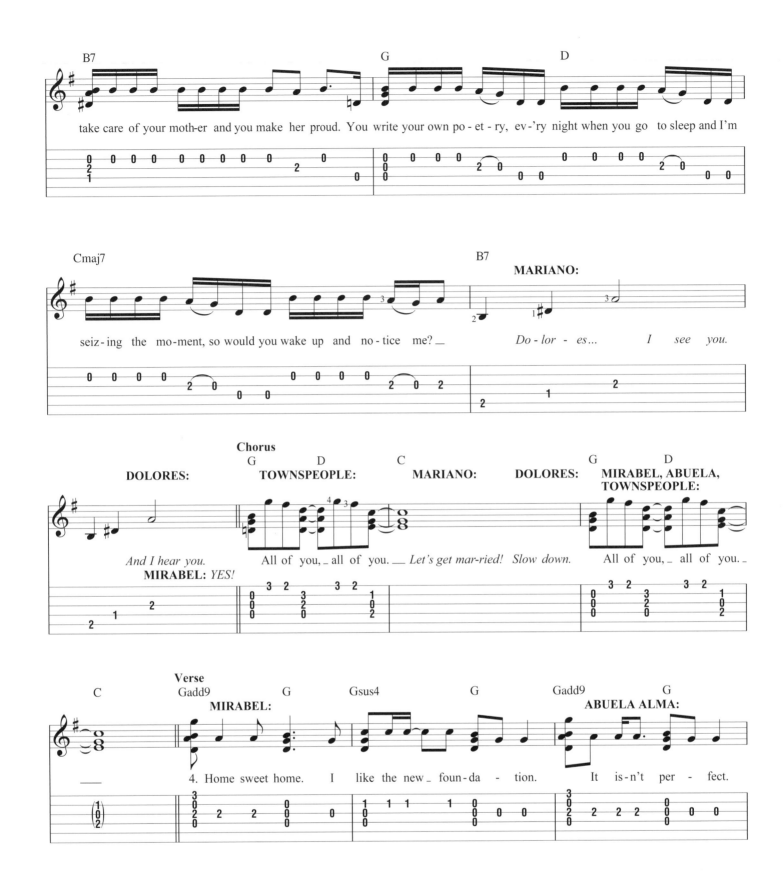

We need a door - knob. *We made this one for you...*

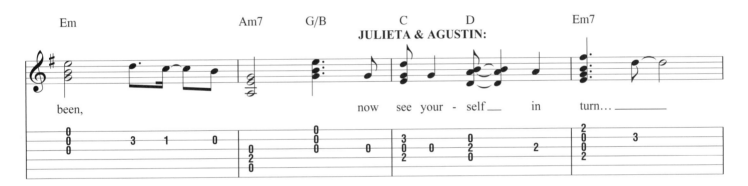

Pre-Chorus 1
DOLORES, PEPA, CAMILO & FÉLIX:

ISABELA & LUISA:

We see how bright_ you burn, we see how brave_ you've

JULIETA & AGUSTIN:

been, now see your - self_ in turn... _

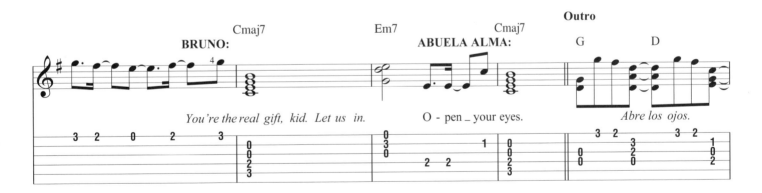

Outro

BRUNO:

ABUELA ALMA:

You're the real gift, kid. Let us in. O - pen _ your eyes. *Abre los ojos.*

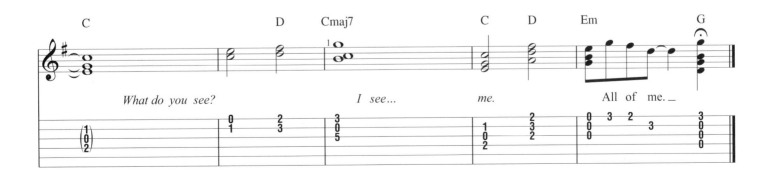

What do you see? *I see...* *me.* All of me. _

Two Oruguitas

Music and Lyrics by Lin-Manuel Miranda

C Em C7 F Fm E

Am G G7 Fmaj7 Gsus4

Strum Pattern: 4
Pick Pattern: 6

Intro
Moderately, in 2

mp

Verse

C

1. Two *or - u-gui - tas* In love and yearn - ing,
2. Two *or - u-gui - tas* A-gainst the weath - er.

C7

Spend ev - 'ry eve - ning and morn - ing learn - ing To hold each oth - er,
The wind grows cold - er, But they're to - geth - er They hold each oth - er,

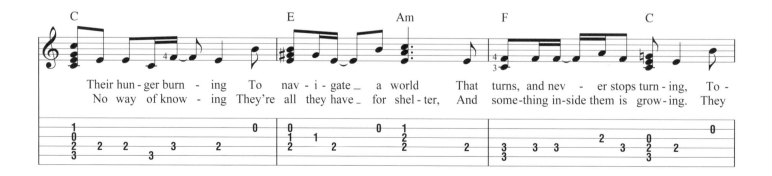

C

Their hun - ger burn - ing To nav - i - gate _ a world That turns, and nev - er stops turn - ing, To -
No way of know - ing They're all they have _ for shel - ter, And some - thing in - side them is grow - ing. They

geth - er in ___ this world   That turns, and nev - er stops turn - ing.

long to stay ___ to - geth - er, But some-thing in-side them is grow - ing.

Ay, ___ *or - u - gui - tas,*

Don't ___ you hold on   too   tight. Both ___ of you know It's your time to grow   To fall a-part, to re - u -nite.

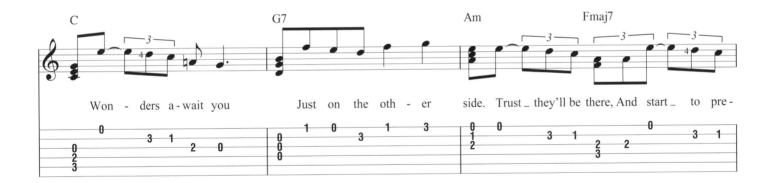

Won - ders a - wait you   Just on the oth - er   side. Trust ___ they'll be there, And start ___ to pre -

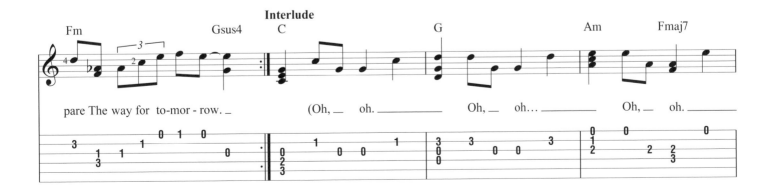

pare The way for to - mor - row. ___   (Oh, ___ oh. _____   Oh, ___ oh... _____   Oh, ___ oh. _____

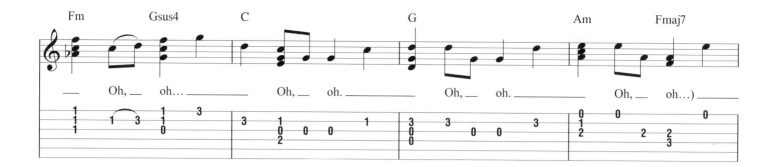

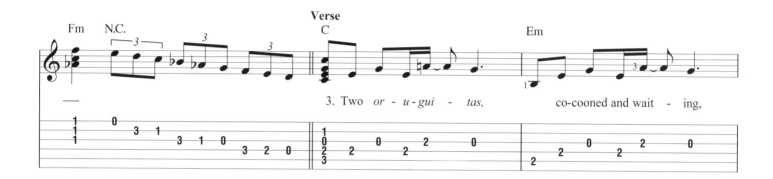

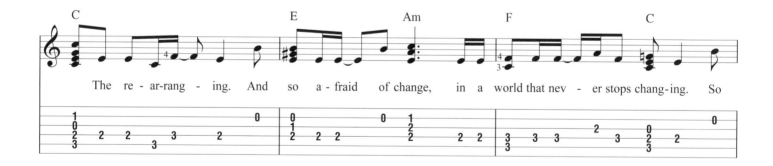

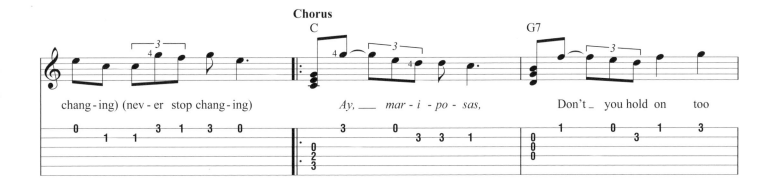

changing) (nev - er stop chang-ing)   Ay, ___ mar - i - po - sas,   Don't ___ you hold on   too

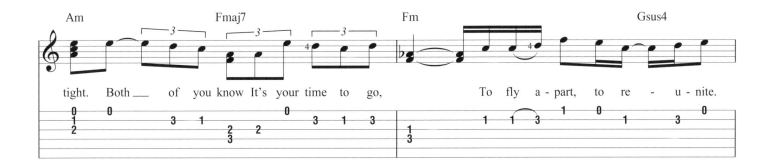

tight. Both ___ of you know It's your time to go,   To fly a - part, to re - u - nite.

Won - ders sur-round you,   Just let the walls come down. Don't ___ look be-hind you, Fly ___ 'til you

find Your way toward to - mor - row ___   find Your way toward to - mor - row. ___